Date: 1/26/22

TOOLS FOR CAREGIVERS

- **F&P LEVEL:** D
- **WORD COUNT:** 55

- **CURRICULUM CONNECTIONS:** animals, habitats

Skills to Teach

- **HIGH-FREQUENCY WORDS:** a, has, her, in, is, it, its, on, the, they, this, too, we
- **CONTENT WORDS:** baby, back, black, call, claws, eat, fur, good, gray, help, joey, koala(s), leaves, live, Mom, night, nose, pouch, rides, sleep, trees, walks
- **PUNCTUATION:** exclamation point, periods
- **WORD STUDY:** /k/, spelled c (*call, claws*); long /a/, spelled ay (*gray*); long /e/, spelled ea (*eat, leaves*); long /e/, spelled ee (*sleep, trees*); /ow/, spelled ou (*pouch*)
- **TEXT TYPE:** factual description

Before Reading Activities

- Read the title and give a simple statement of the main idea.
- Have students "walk" through the book and talk about what they see in the pictures.
- Introduce new vocabulary by having students predict the first letter and locate the word in the text.
- Discuss any unfamiliar concepts that are in the text.

After Reading Activities

Ask the readers to flip back through the book. What features do koalas have that help them live in trees? How might claws help them grip branches? How might keeping a baby in a pouch help a koala mom as she moves through the trees? Ask the readers: If you could have one animal feature, what would it be and why?

Tadpole Books are published by Jump!, 5357 Penn Avenue South, Minneapolis, MN 55419, www.jumplibrary.com

Editor: Jenna Gleisner Designer: Molly Ballanger

Photo Credits: Eric Isselee/Shutterstock, cover, 2br, 8–9; GlobalP/iStock, 1; Suzi Eszterhas/Minden Pictures/SuperStock, 2tr, 2mr, 3, 12–13; Raimund Linke/age fotostock/SuperStock, 2ml, 4–5; Andras Deak/Shutterstock, 2tl, 2bl, 6–7, 10–11; markrhiggins/iStock, 14–15; Marianne Purdie/Dreamstime, 16.

Library of Congress Cataloging-in-Publication Data
Names: Nilsen, Genevieve, author.
Title: Koala joeys / by Genevieve Nilsen.
Description: Minneapolis: Jump!, Inc., 2022. | Series: Outback babies | Includes index. | Audience: Ages 3–6
Identifiers: LCCN 2020047816 (print) | LCCN 2020047817 (ebook) | ISBN 9781645279495 (hardcover)
ISBN 9781645279501 (paperback) | ISBN 9781645279518 (ebook)
Subjects: LCSH: Koala—Infancy—Juvenile literature.
Classification: LCC QL737.M384 N55 2022 (print) | LCC QL737.M384 (ebook) | DDC 599.2/51392—dc23
LC record available at https://lccn.loc.gov/2020047816
LC ebook record available at https://lccn.loc.gov/2020047817

KOALA JOEYS

by Genevieve Nilsen

TABLE OF CONTENTS

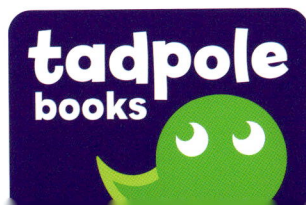

tadpole books

WORDS TO KNOW

claws

eat

fur

joey

pouch

rides

KOALA JOEYS

joey

This baby is a koala.
We call it a joey.

3

The joey has gray fur.

4

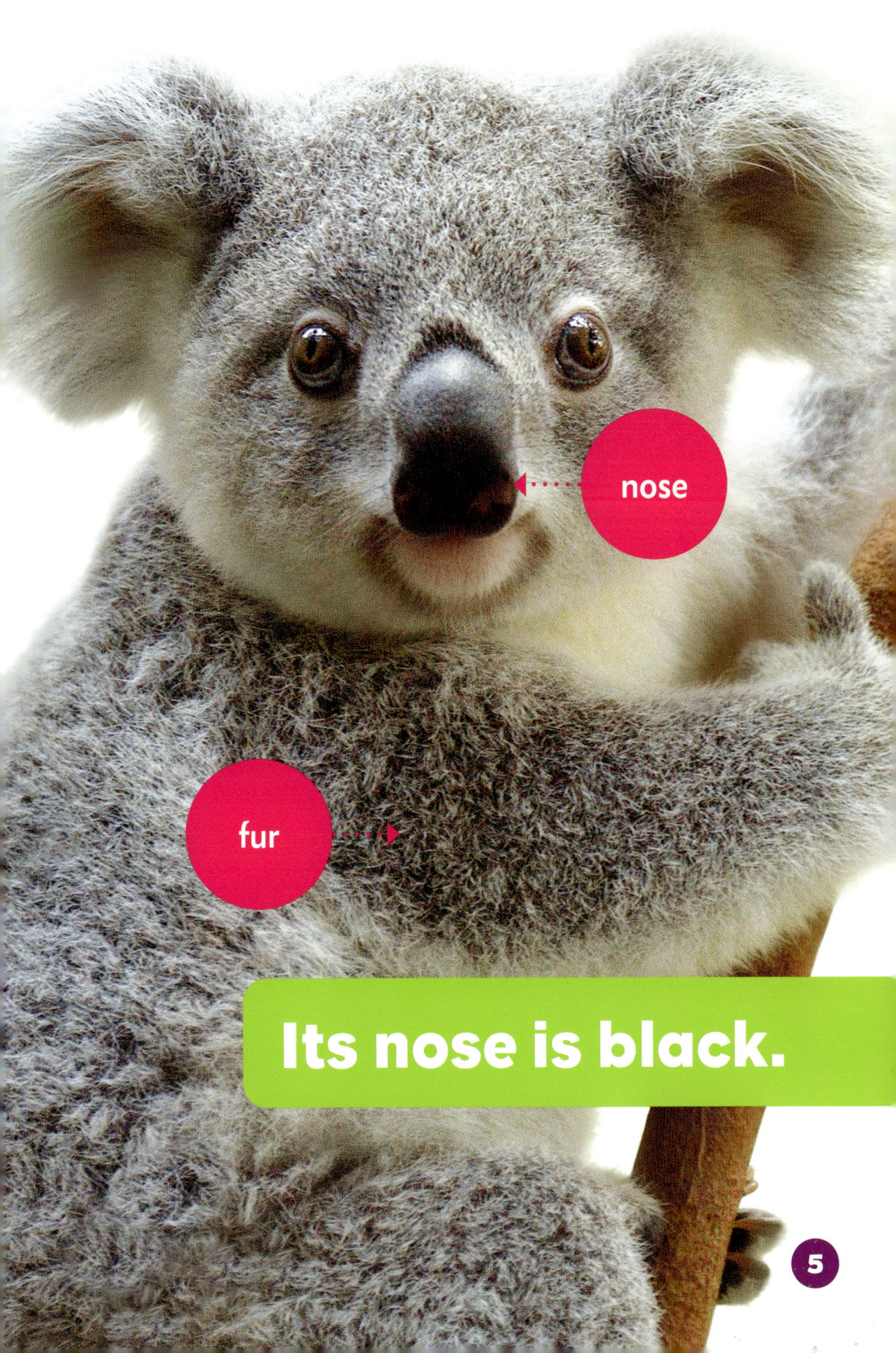

nose

fur

Its nose is black.

pouch

Mom has a pouch.

6

The joey rides in it.

The joey rides on her back, too.

The joey walks.

claw

Claws help.

leaf

Koalas live in trees.

They eat leaves.

13

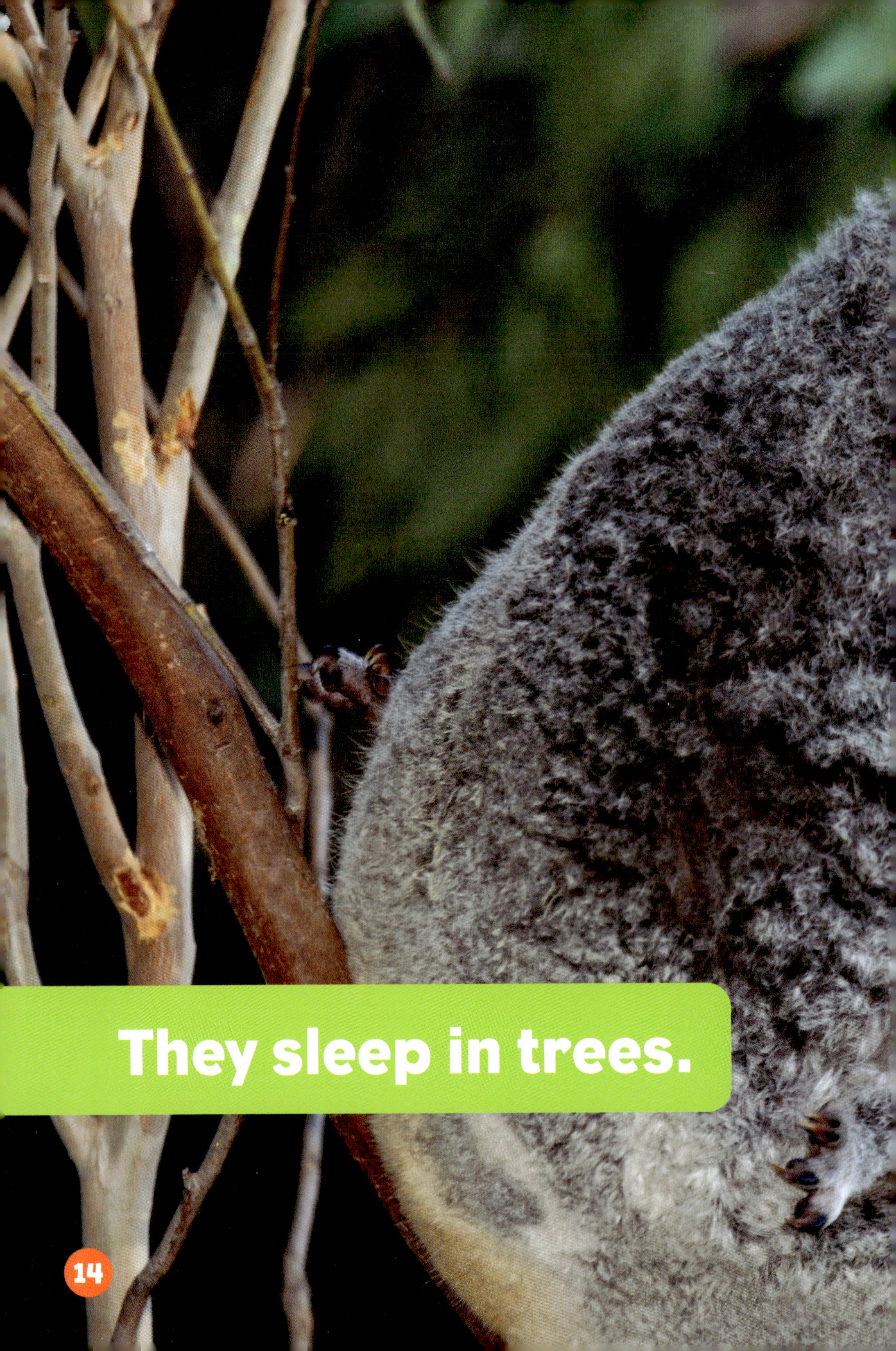

They sleep in trees.

Good night!

LET'S REVIEW!

What is this koala joey doing?

INDEX

16